10 Fundraising Ideas & Strategies

by Alex Genadinik

ISBN:1-50-237835-4
ISBN-13: 978-1-50-237835-4

DEDICATION

Dedicated to my mother and grandmother who are the biggest entrepreneurs I know.

CONTENTS

FOREWORD

Dear reader,

Nice to meet you! I appreciate that you got this book. Before we get started, I want to explain why I wrote this book, how I decided on the chapters and sections, and where the knowledge comes from, and how you can read the book to get the most out of it. This will help us be on the same page throughout the book, and you will know what to expect.

I am a software engineer by trade, entrepreneur via life's winding roads, and a pursuer of my own curiosities by inclination. I've been coming up with business ideas since college. Many of my early ideas were ridiculous, some absurd, and a few I still adore that just didn't work as a business. I was able to bring many of my business ideas to life on the web because I was able to create software. Along the way, I've had many failures (ouch!) and successes. One success in particular led me to write this book.

I released my first mobile app in April 2012. It was an Android business planning app that eventually evolved into a series of apps called the Problemio apps on iPhone and Android. On each platform, the apps come as a 4-app business series covering business ideas, business planning, fundraising, and marketing. Most of the apps are free. Together, the apps have over 2,000,000 downloads and have become the foundation on which I've built my greater business. In addition to the apps, I eventually wrote 20+ books on business and marketing topics, built a business that coaches business owners, and created 100+ online business and marketing courses. As a token of my appreciation for purchasing this book, I will provide you with a free course of your choosing. See the Further Resources section for more information.

I can attribute almost everything that came after I launched my initial app to one early app feature. That feature was me personally offering free business advice right on the apps via text chat to anyone with questions.

Since only a fraction of app users asked for advice back when the apps were averaging under 100 daily downloads, it was easy for me to handle the volume of questions. However, when the apps had around 500 downloads per day, it became impossible for me to handle all the queries. I would often not be able to sleep because questions were coming in throughout the night, and I was anxious and excited to help people. After the apps started getting over 1,000 daily downloads, I made coaching paid in order to reduce demand. I had to stop spending so much time helping customers they didn't pay because in addition to answering all those questions, I had to spend my time developing and marketing the app.

I still help people every day, and over the years, I've brought my care and passion to help over 2,000 entrepreneurs on a one-on-one basis. Based on that vast experience of helping people who are starting their businesses, since you are likely just starting your own business, I understand exactly what kind of help you need, and the kinds of questions you might want to ask.

Guess what kinds of questions I get asked most frequently by entrepreneurs. Almost all entrepreneurs ask about how they can raise money for their business!

That led me to look far and wide and come up with the 10 different strategies to raise money. Many of the fundraising strategies in this book are ones that I worked on with my clients to help them raise money while some of the strategies are fraught with pitfalls. Since my involvement with my clients was hands-on, I have direct experience with almost all the fundraising strategies in this book, which makes the advice much stronger. The advice in this book is based on practical experience. I am excited to share it with you so let's get started.

I hope you'll find the book interesting, insightful, and helpful for your business so that your entrepreneurial journey can be a little easier. Enjoy.

CHAPTER 1: BASICS OF RAISING MONEY

1. Are you excited to work hard?

Congratulations, you are an entrepreneur. Hustle and hard work are now your way of life.

Ideally, I could help you find a button you could press on some website to have money come out of your computer like an ATM machine. Unfortunately, in the absence of that magic button, raising money is almost always about pure hustle.

Almost every strategy in this book comes down to one theme: sitting back and waiting for money to come to you won't work. But if you hustle, work hard, be resourceful, creative, and persistent, you *will* get the money you're seeking. I need you to fully understand that the greatest key to your fundraising success is your hard work. The level of effort you put into your fundraising will have a direct correlation to your success.

You likely just thought something like "I am motivated and excited. I'm ready to work hard and hustle and blah blah blah." Excitement is good. You should be excited, but in the beginning, everyone is highly motivated, excited, and says that they will work hard. But business and fundraising isn't a sprint. It is more of a marathon that has many sprints in it. Business is like a sport where there are nearly no rules and every once in a while someone or something blindsides you with a club, but despite that, you have to keep moving forward. So for now, put these words into your mental back pocket: persistence, consistency, creativity, resourcefulness, scrappy, hard work, work-life balance.

Just kidding about work-life balance. I really got you there, didn't I? Work-life balance as people traditionally think of it is for later. For entrepreneurs, work-life balance is the extra enjoyment and fulfillment that we get from our work, with the need for work-life balance naturally decreasing.

In the beginning, you better be all hustle. Hustle will be a theme throughout this book. It has to be. If I told you it's easy to raise money, I would be lying.

Hope you are still excited because it would be sad if the excitement waned before finishing the first section of the first chapter.

The field of Emotional Intelligence teaches us that excitement is important to boost your short-term motivation. But excitement is a short-lived emotion that can't carry us far forward. In addition to short-term excitement, you need long-term motivation to keep you working on your business every day for months and years to come. Channel your initial excitement to get started, but also find the intrinsic motivators that drew you to your business. Intrinsic motivation will keep you motivated long-term, and help you hunker down and do some serious work over the long haul.

2. How much money should you raise to start your business?

Before raising money, you must understand how much money your business actually needs. I know you'd take as much as possible, but you can't say that to an investor or a bank. You must have a figure in mind. Your strategy might be very different if you need $1,000 or $50,000 or $1,000,000. Knowing the exact amount of money you need to raise will help you set achievable and realistic fundraising goals and choose the strategies most likely to work.

Let's cover the concept of cash flow analysis which helps you calculate how much money your business requires. Cash flow analysis is a process of determining how cash "flows" in and out of your business. Unfortunately, in the beginning it mostly flows out. Crying emoticon goes here.

Performing a cash flow analysis for large businesses can be quite complex and should be done by an accountant. For small businesses, a cash flow analysis is relatively simple; it only sounds intimidating. Since you are most likely just starting your project, your cash flow statement will be nothing more than a relatively short itemized list of expenses and revenue that comes in.

If you have not yet started your business, I recommend creating two cash flow statements. The first statement should focus on the cash flows before you launch, and the second should focus on ongoing cash flows after you launch.

To simplify things even further, let's first focus on itemizing the costs. Most costs can be predicted with reasonable accuracy. It helps to have someone on your team with prior experience growing a business in your industry. Their experience will help you make a more accurate projection of expenses. If your team does not have direct experience in your chosen industry, it isn't the end of the world. You can accurately predict your costs using these three things:

1) **Common sense**: Think ahead and list the expenses you can think of that you might incur during the start-up process before you launch and on an ongoing basis. Many items are quite obvious. Some examples of expenses are as simple as paying rent, employee salary, utility bills, legal setup fees, etc.

2) **Coaching**: Hire a coach or mentor who has experience succeeding with a similar business. They can easily identify what additional expenses your business might incur. For most businesses, hiring a coach for this process should not be expensive as it should take less than an hour for a true expert to list 90% of the possible start-up costs.

3) **Research**: Reach out to vendors to get price quotes for items like rent of your office space or equipment.

You will have a very clear picture of your start-up costs through this simple process. However, since things rarely go exactly as planned, you might want to give yourself some wiggle room and increase your original projections by 50-100% of your original expense calculation.

Now let's discuss costs after you launch your business. That calculation is similar to the one we just covered except it has one caveat. You need to give yourself a "runway," which is the first 0-12 months of your business operating at a loss after launch. Few businesses start out profitably, so you have to project your expenses into the future.

For this calculation, just add the costs to start and keep your business afloat for the first 0 to 12 months. Choose the time you think it will take you to break even. The approximate time range should be based on the type of your business and the average time it takes for a business like yours to break even. Add the expenses projected over the time you think you will need to break even and you will have your projected costs.

Luckily, you don't need to raise enough money to get to break-even. You need to raise enough money to get to a MILESTONE.

In addition to profitability after which you can stop fundraising, a milestone can be a point after which it might become easier to raise more money. Some examples of milestones are the launch of your business, first 1,000 website sign-ups, a certain number of paying customers, or anything else that is a sign of business progress or growth.

When making a fundraising plan, you can choose to raise enough money to get to a realistic milestone from which it will be possible to raise more money.

Now that you know how to count the costs to get to a milestone, you know what amount to specifically request when asked how much money you need to raise. Simple, right?

After you launch your business, you will finally have

cash flows *into* your business and not just out of it. This is money that comes into your business via revenue streams and will offset the costs.

It is more difficult to accurately predict the revenue that you may earn than it is to predict the costs. Generating revenue and sales will be up to you. You can generate zero or millions of dollars.

The art here is to predict the realistic revenue for your situation. That largely comes from industry experience or getting the right coaching or mentoring. Again, it is prudent to add a cushion on top of your estimated financial needs because during the planning phase, entrepreneurs tend to be overly optimistic about how things will go, and underestimate the challenges.

Once you've calculated how much money you need to raise, you can begin looking into ways of doing so. Most people choose to only pursue one way to raise money, but you can use more than one fundraising source to cobble together your necessary amount, which is why this book gives you a bevy of options.

Some common sources of funding are loans, grants, investments, donations, revenue of your actual business, creative fundraising techniques, and getting the money up-front from potential customers. Additionally, if you are based in the United States, you can check government sites like grants.gov or sba.gov to see if any help is available for entrepreneurs in your specific situation. If you are not based in the United

States, there are probably equivalent sites for your country. Just look up what those are for wherever you are based.

You might wonder what happens if you can't raise the money you need to start your business. Unfortunately, despite many options, most people never raise money to start their businesses. This causes many to abandon their dreams, but it doesn't have to be that way. As a part of your business planning, you can either amend your original idea to start smaller and require less money, or embrace bootstrapping.

3. Bootstrapping: How to start your business without much money

An overwhelming number of entrepreneurs who write to me ask how they can start a business if they have no money to put into it and no possibility of raising that money.

Most entrepreneurs face the problem of not having enough money to accomplish the things he or she needs in order to grow their business. You are not alone. I realize that every day spent without money might feel like an eternity, but don't lose confidence. Just be resourceful and figure out how to get around your money issues. History shows that it is completely possible to overcome not having much money to start your business. It is obviously much simpler to start a business if you have money, but people create successful businesses without much money all the time. In fact, going through that experience will make you a much stronger entrepreneur. The number one factor in determining the success of your business is not money, but your effort, persistence, resourcefulness, and creative problem solving. So, let's start with bootstrapping and what that means for your business.

The definition of bootstrapping is the process of starting a self-sustaining business that is supposed to proceed without external financial input. Such businesses are typically funded by the founder or are able to quickly generate revenue from customers.

Few people bootstrap because they want to. Most entrepreneurs are forced into it out of financial necessity. But it can be a blessing in disguise because it forces the entrepreneur to take on a can-do attitude which helps accomplish many things cheaply or for free.

Let me share my own experience as a case study and an example. I bootstrapped my mobile app business and never raised money for it. Did I wish I could just raise the funds I needed? Of course. But money didn't just come to me so I had to either kill the idea or make it happen with the limited resources I had. Even if you don't have a cent to your name, you always have your hands and your brain. I could not hire employees, could not pay for a nice design for my apps, had to build the product by myself, had to learn to do marketing and sales, and do everything else that the business required. Since I didn't have a co-founder or a business partner who could help me with some of those tasks, I had to learn many of the necessary skills to get them done.

Of course, it is impossible for anyone to do many of the tasks needed in a business to a high degree of quality. For example, design was a very difficult thing for me to learn, and I wasn't able to do it on my own. But I was able to quickly get up to speed with most tasks/skills needed by the business and implement them to approximately 60-70% of the quality of a professional. Most of the time, that was either enough or made hiring the professional much cheaper because they didn't have to do the work from scratch. Plus, over time, I continued to improve my skills, and because I had my back against the wall, I became as good as a professional in many necessary crafts. Marketing is an example of such a skill because if I did not become good at it, the business would not have survived.

Learning new skills instead of outsourcing them is admittedly a much slower and more frustrating way of completing tasks than giving those tasks to a professional and getting a polished result back quickly. But it has its long-term advantages because it requires less cash and less time spent on hiring and management because you don't have to ask anyone for help. Having acquired many skills, I can now quickly complete multiple tasks and not have any delays due to waiting for anyone or having to explain to someone what I need.

Even if you raise money, you can't outsource everything. There is always a balance of how much you can do on your own and how much you hire out. Supplement whatever money you end up gathering with your own hard work and hunger to learn new skills. That hybrid approach is ideal. As your business grows, you will do less on your own and hire for more tasks, but at the starting phase of most companies, it is inevitable that you will need to learn many skills instead of throwing cash at every challenge.

4. Ramen Profitability

For many businesses, the real milestone is simply to break even financially on a month-to-month basis. That is when a gigantic part of the stress goes away and you are able to breathe more easily. I remember that moment myself. It is a feeling of decreased financial stress, which had been impacting every facet of my life. A layer of heaviness and worry was lifted.

Paul Graham of the Y Combinator described the term "ramen profitability" as a time when you can limit your expenses so much that if you survive on just ramen noodles, you can cover your living expenses with the revenue of your business. I've always felt that this analogy is brilliant. The brilliance of this analogy is easiest to see when you imagine just how different almost every day and moment of your life will be from how it is when you are in a financial freefall.

5. Types of businesses and their common sources of fundraising

To help you understand which fundraising strategies might work for you, I came up with a list of strategies that typically work for each type of business.

i. **Growth businesses (often apps, tech, or start-ups)**: These companies usually raise money from professional growth seed investors, crowdfunding, friends and family, incubators

ii. **Local businesses**: These companies usually raise money from savings, friends and family, non-professional investors

iii. **Self-branded or single-entrepreneur lifestyle businesses**: These companies usually raise money from self-funding, friends and family, or ideally from revenue

iv. **Nonprofits**: These organizations usually raise money from grants, crowdfunding, savings, friends and family

v. **Agency or service provider (like design or**

app/software development or marketing services): These companies usually raise money from self-funding, savings, and friends and family

6. Your fundraising story

It helps to have a compelling fundraising narrative. This can be a story you present that explains why your business is interesting/unique/necessary. This ties into your milestone, your targeted fundraising source (your story can change a little with each fundraising source), and the kind of business you have.

For example, if you are raising money from investors, you need to sell them on growth and billion-dollar potential. If you are soliciting money from friends and family, they have to identify with your story on an emotional level and trust you with their money. If you are crowdfunding from a mass audience of people who don't know you, you not only need to have people connect with your story on an emotional level but also need to make your project appear as necessary in the world and very cool or go viral.

CHAPTER 2: THE 10 FUNDRAISING SOURCES

1. Loans

Many entrepreneurs try to get small business loans to fund their businesses. The problem is that you are risking money that you don't even have by receiving that business loan. You are doubling the risk of putting your savings into your business because if the business fails, you will still need to pay back that loan and interest on top of that.

In most situations, I try to talk people out of taking large business loans to start their company. Once the business has grown, loans are a more viable option to finance business operations. But it is very different if you have not started yet and are looking to get a loan to start.

For those who still want to get a loan to start their business, let's cover how to get one, the difference between taking a personal loan and applying it to your business vs. getting an actual business loan, and a few other details.

Banks Do Not Grant Business Loans to Companies That Have Not Started

Many people looking to get a loan think they can apply for a bank loan. Unfortunately, banks do not loan to businesses that have not started because it is too risky for the bank. Banks like predictability. It is nearly impossible to predict how a business concept will do in the future, especially given the fact that statistically most businesses fail. Large banks often require businesses to be in operation for two or more years and generate thousands of dollars in monthly revenue before considering that company for a loan. Smaller, regional banks may have fewer requirements, but they often still require the business be operational and have proof of revenue.

Microloans Under $100,000 and Crowd-Lending

There are a number of options for getting a microloan. Most microloans tend to be under $100,000. Some microloan companies are Kiva, Lendio and Prosper, and a few others. Each of these microloan companies work in slightly different ways. In many cases, they still prefer to lend to businesses that have already started and have a track record, but it might be possible to get a loan if you have good credit history.

Lendio works by matching you with potential lenders according your credit history, business type, location, and a number of other factors. To get matched with a lender, all a person has to do is fill out a form on Lendio. And if you are eligible for a loan, Lendio contacts you with further details and instructions for getting that loan from a lender with whom you are matched.

Prosper works by crowd-sourcing lending. For example, instead of finding a single lender for thousands of dollars, Prosper can gather small sums from many lenders to loan you the money.

Personal Loans vs. Business Loans

When people cannot get a business loan, they can sometimes take out a personal loan and put that money toward starting their business. Bear in mind that this increases your personal risk.

If you take out a business loan and your business cannot pay it back, you are not personally liable for that loan in most cases, the business is liable. However, if you take out a personal loan to apply to the business, you are personally liable for paying back that loan and your credit history will suffer if you are not able to do so. Also, remember, banks are not naive; they often have legal ways to go after you personally even if the loan is a business loan.

Pros And Cons Of Getting a Business Loan

There are some strong opponents of getting business loans to fund your business. One is an investor and entrepreneur named Marc Cuban who believes that since many businesses fail, most people will need to pay back the loan. So it is not any different than spending your own money. And people often take out much bigger loans than they can realistically afford to lose. Marc is a big proponent of paying back any outstanding personal loans you may have, saving your money, and spending some of your savings to get your business started.

Loans aren't all bad. The advantage of being able to get a loan is that just like anything else, it is another weapon in your arsenal. Sometimes, it is the right tool. When people need a small amount of money that is perhaps under $20,000, getting a small loan can help them get started, especially if they can't easily get grants or investments. So a small loan might be the right option for them in that instance. Of course, they would need a way to pay that loan back, having the option to be able to get a loan is a good option that is the right one in some cases.

There is a range in the $3,000 to $20,000 amount where many types of businesses can't get started if they don't have the money, and that money goes a disproportionately long way to get people started. Some examples of such situations are when the entrepreneur needs to buy initial equipment to perform some work or a truck. Getting the money would allow them to start immediately instead of going through weeks or months of fundraising efforts.

Is It Possible to Get a Business Loan With Bad Credit?

If you have bad credit history, it is more difficult to get a business loan. Luckily, some lenders will look at the health of your overall business instead, and if the business is going well, that might compensate for your bad credit history.

Here is a list of companies where you can potentially get a loan:

- http://www.lendingclub.com
- http://www.prosper.com
- http://www.sofi.com
- http://www.lendio.com
- http://www.upstart.com
- http://www.kiva.org

There are also many credit repair strategies out there that you can either research and implement on your own, or hire a credit repair firm to help you bring your credit score back up.

2. Grants

Many entrepreneurs hope to get a grant to fund their small business because it sounds like free money, but the truth is that getting a grant is quite difficult. Not everyone is even eligible. And even when people are eligible for a certain grant, they must compete with other organizations that are also trying to get that grant. The success rate of getting a grant to fund a small business is very low due to high competition and the fact that most loans are given to nonprofits rather than for-profit businesses.

Grant Eligibility

If you are based in the U.S., visit the United States grant eligibility page or grants.gov to determine if you qualify. If you are not based in U.S., find the equivalent website for your country.

Grants are generally available to government organizations, educational organizations, public housing organizations, and nonprofits. Small for-profit businesses can also be eligible for grants, but that is less common. Individuals can also be eligible to get grants, but again, that is less common. An individual can also apply for grants on their own behalf, and not on behalf of a company, organization, institution, or government. Individuals sign the grant application and its associated certifications and assurances that are necessary to fulfill the requirements.

Sources for Grants

When you research for grants, investigate whether there are any grants available from organizations or communities to which you belong. If you are a part of a minority, there may be grants available to that minority. If you are a member of a religious group, there may be grants for members of that religious group. The same is true for any community you may belong to. Additionally, cities and even particular neighborhoods always try to stimulate local business growth. Search if those types of grants are available in your local area.

3. Investors

The next source to consider is raising money from investors. Investors come in many different shapes and sizes. They tend to have different methodologies and philosophies for how they like to invest. One good resource to find technology investors is AngelList.com. Technology investors typically look for proven teams, high growth, and billion-dollar markets. Most businesses do not fit that profile. Funding your company by getting an investment is almost always difficult. Nevertheless, here are some options and tips for doing so.

Note: The below breakdown applies to investments in

technology, and <u>not</u> businesses like common local services, restaurants, gyms, or other types of small businesses.

Investment From Friends and Family

You can get an investment from friends and family if your business is in a very early stage or even the planning stage. Most professional investors might be hesitant to invest in a venture that is too new and founded by a first-time entrepreneur. So your friends and family might be a good source for raising an initial small investment to get your business off the ground.

Many people do not like to get their friends and family involved in their business because they not want to risk those relationships, but they are an easy and convenient resource for an investment.

Seed Stage Investments

Seed stage investments are typically made by professional investors. These investments can range from $25,000 to $750,000 depending on many factors. To get a seed stage investment, you typically need have already started your business and demonstrate some type of growth and product adoption. The website AngelList.com has a big list of seed stage investors. You can browse their bios and the kinds of businesses and niches they like to invest in. If one matches your business, figure out a way to reach out to them and get your start-up in front of them.

Start-up Incubators

Various start-up incubators also give seed stage investments, and typically don't require a company to have already been started (although it is a plus if a company can show some traction). Incubators typically look for groundbreaking businesses in large, popular or new markets.

Amazingly, AngelList.com also has a large list of start-up incubators:

https://angel.co/incubators

Angel Stage Investments

This kind of investment can overlap with seed stage investing. The overlap is both in the types of investors who invest at this stage, and the amounts of money that is put in. Angel investments tend to be slightly bigger than seed stage investments, and typically go to businesses that can demonstrate more market adoption.

Series A, B, and C Stage Venture Capital Investments

There is a lot of talk of raising venture capital, but the truth is that very few companies can ever be considered for this type of an investment. Venture capitalists require steady and phenomenal growth, a gigantic target market, and a slew of other factors. Most companies never qualify for venture money, but that is not necessarily a bad thing. Raising venture capital can hurt a company because it limits your options. Venture capitalists want fast growth and to shoot big. That might sound nice, but their money often comes with many unneeded pressures that can do considerable damage to your company. Plus, in many cases, if things don't go their way, they can have the founding CEO replaced.

Where You Can Go Wrong

Many people want to get an investment too early in the development of their business. There are a few problems with that. First of all, the earlier you are in the process, the less likely you will get funding. Most of the time when people try to get an investment for their company too-early, they just waste their time that could be better spent trying to actually grow the company.

Another problem with seeking an investment too early is that even in the unlikely event that an investment is secured, the deal will probably favor the investor. Thus the entrepreneur will get very poor deal terms and give up a larger portion of ownership than they would if they got the investment when their business was more mature.

Additionally, be careful of bad investors or of taking money from someone who may not be a good fit for the company you are trying to grow. Investors should bring more than just cash; they should bring connections, mentoring, and industry expertise.

The Best Time to Seek an Investment

There are many conflicting theories on the best time to get an investment. One theory suggests taking the money whenever you can get it because you never know when the economy might change for the worse. Another theory suggests that you should seek investment when you have a proven company with market traction.

If you are struggling financially, raising money can help you relieve an immense amount of stress. But if you can hold off on raising money, wait until you've reached a point where you can give up less equity and take a bigger investment. If you can make the investors feel like the train is leaving the station and they better get on the train soon, that is the ideal time to raise money from investors.

The most frustrating part of raising money from investors is that they are usually not there to invest in your business when you are struggling the most. But once you've done the tough part and made your business able to stand on its own, and grow, and need investors less, they become more readily available.

4. Donations

The next item on our list is raising money via donations. Donations can be raised in a few ways. You can open a nonprofit to raise donations using the old-fashioned way of mailing or calling past customers or donors. If your nonprofit is a charity, you can raise money by seeking donations from wealthy individuals who use donations to get tax write-offs.

Another way to get donations is through crowdfunding. Crowdfunding is relatively new and is popular in tech-savvy crowds, but it is still a bit mystifying to most people outside of the tech and social media world.

Crowdfunding takes advantage of the power of the Internet and allows anyone to donate to a project they believe in or are excited by. That is great for the entrepreneur starting the project because it gives them some free money with nearly no strings attached.

Crowdfunding is rapidly growing, and many projects have already raised hundreds of thousands or millions of dollars via this method. The leading crowdfunding site is Kickstarter.com.

Raising Donations Via Crowdfunding On Kickstarter

A site called Kickstarter.com is the leader in this space. Originally they only allowed art projects to get funded, but now allow a broad range of projects. Their rules do frequently change to accommodate their growth and the evolving laws around crowdfunding. For their current terms of service, and to see if you are eligible to apply, check their site.

Raising Donations Via Crowdfunding With Indiegogo

The second biggest crowdfunding site is indiegogo.com, which is essentially a slightly smaller version of Kickstarter. Kickstarter allows a more narrow range of projects than Indiegogo. So if for some reason Kickstarter does not accept your project, you can use Indiegogo.

Both KickStarter and Indiegogo charge a small fee for projects that reach their fundraising goal. The caveat is that on both these sites, if you don't reach your fundraising goal within the allowed time, you do not get any of the money you raised.

Raising Donations Via Crowdfunding With GoFundMe

GoFundMe isn't one of the leaders in this space, but is one of the most flexible crowdfunding sites. There is no deadline or cutoff date for a particular campaign, it can be perpetual, and there are no restrictions on the type of projects allowed on the site.

Specialized Crowdfunding Sites

There are also many other crowdfunding sites that specialize in funding various niches. For example, AppStori specialized in crowdfunding for mobile apps and Petridish specialized in crowdfunding for science projects. Unfortunately both are now defunct but if you are interested in crowdfunding, search for a niche crowdfunding site that may work best for your type of project and industry.

It is often easier to get more attention on niche crowdfunding sites, and the people looking to donate on those sites are more likely to take an interest in your project. The main problem with niche crowdfunding sites is that they are often too small and you can't raise too much money from them.

Some crowdfunding sites are more effective than others at raising money, so you have to judge what is right for you based on the nature of your project and your funding needs. If you want to give it a try, you need to understand how crowdfunding really works.

How Crowdfunding Really Works: The Inside Scoop

Entrepreneurs hope to attract new potential donors when posting on crowdfunding sites; however, it often requires that the entrepreneur invite friends to the site to donate. So, in essence, the fundraising entrepreneur has to do an enormous amount of promotion in order to spread the word anyway. The site merely acts as a platform and centralized, secure location for the donations. This might be misleading if you expect to post your project and have money to magically appear. Crowdfunding works by having you—the person raising money—actively promote your crowdfunding campaign.

Additionally, most crowdfunding sites take a small percentage of the total money raised.

5. Part-time or full-time work

Let's consider what happens if you get a full-time or part-time job to fund your business. A job allows you to save between few hundred and a few thousand dollars a month. It also gives you a chance to learn about an industry that's potentially the same as your business. That makes this a good option because you can be getting paid to learn your industry.

The challenge is that most people can't raise tens or hundreds of thousands of dollars this way. But I personally funded my Problemio mobile apps business by working and saving money. That allowed me to not have to rely on sources like investors, and I was able to remain independent. This is an underrated but good option to fund your business. I've personally used it with success.

6. Money from the revenue of the business

Earning revenue with your business sooner rather than later is a great way to fund your business. This approach to funding your company is the best long-term path to sustain your business without having to rely on investors or other outside sources. Additionally, this is the most natural way for your business to raise money.

If you raise money from loans or investors, that fundraising process has nothing to do with running your actual business. But if you raise money through your company's revenue, that effort has everything to do with getting your actual business to function properly because you will be putting your business on a course on which it ultimately has to be on anyway.

I should add that after I saved the money to fund my business, I focused on generating revenue as soon as I could so that the business could sustain itself. This isn't easy to do. The advantage of this approach is that there is no wasted effort during the fundraising process. Everything you do aligns your business to naturally generate more money from its operations.

7. Creative ways to raise money

Sometimes you can raise money by doing something creative. Here is one example. A few years ago, I was trying to grow a group hiking website as a business. It was difficult, and I never raised money for it from investors, donations, or any other sources. It was 100% bootstrapped. To get attention for the website, I started organizing cool hiking events such as hikes to find lost shipwrecks or old cannons that were in the area. By incorporating those themed hikes, I was able to get many people to attend, some of whom I charged money. That turned out to be great for my business. I raised extra cash, met interesting people, and got promotion for my website that resulted in many new customers.

The money I raised this way went a long way to helping me fund the website design and development. It wasn't a lot of money, but it was the boost I needed at that time. And the great thing about organizing events to generate money for your business is that they can happen on a regular basis. Once you find a type of event or theme that works, you can do it over and over.

8. Money up-front from future customers

Here is a case study from a business that raised money from a future customer. There was a company that was building a product for bars and pubs. The founders didn't have the money to fully develop the product so they approached a number of the bar owners and convinced them to put some money toward the development of the product in exchange for a deep discount in the future. That gave these entrepreneurs a way to raise enough money to fund their product development.

You can include such fundraising efforts as early as your business planning process. When you gather feedback about whether people think your business idea is good, if they say they like it, ask them whether they'd become a customer. If they say yes, ask them to do so right then and there for a discount. This won't just help you raise money. This will help you keep the people giving you feedback about your business more honest. It is easy for anyone to say that your business ideas is good. But the truth comes out once people have to put money where their mouth is.

9. Educational classes and workshops

Almost any business has some expertise to share with the rest of their industry or potential clients. Even if the business itself is relatively young, it probably has enough expertise within the founding team that could be beneficial to absolute beginners in that field.

You can turn that expertise into online and offline educational resources. For example, you can hold in-person workshops or classes teaching various things. Online you can create and sell classes on Udemy or Skillshare and earn passive income. You can also write books or make YouTube videos with similar educational material.

All of these strategies will help you earn revenue that you can put toward your business. in addition to revenue, you can get extra brand exposure and leads for your business from your workshops and courses.

10. Provide services online

Whatever your expertise may be, you can generate extra revenue by doing some work online. There are many sites that help you earn money. Some of these are Upwork.com, Fiverr.com, eBay.com, Amazon.com, various other online concierge or coaching websites such as Clarity.fm where experts help entrepreneurs, or any other service marketplace. I'll cover this more in depth in a later chapter. There are many large websites from which you can generate a side income online.

If you enjoy listening to podcasts, my friend Nick Loper runs a very popular weekly podcast called the *Side Hustle Nation* in which he interviews people with unique and interesting ways to make money on the side. If you listen to enough episodes, you can get hundreds of ideas for how to generate extra income online and, in some cases, you may do well enough with those sources that they become your main source of income.

11. BONUS: How to raise money with Cryptocurrency

Note: This section of the book assumes that you are

familiar with Bitcoin and the concept of cryptocurrency. These are relatively new concepts. Many people are not aware of them, and even those who are familiar with these concepts don't fully understand them. Feel free to look at this Wikipedia page for a better understanding:

http://en.wikipedia.org/wiki/Bitcoin

I'll try to briefly explain this concept here as well. Cryptocurrency is a new kind of currency that is all digital. It is traded globally and is not attached to any government (although individual governments place various restrictions on its use). You can buy and sell goods using Bitcoin wherever Bitcoin is accepted. In many ways, it is similar to how you would buy and sell goods using dollars, although Bitcoin is much less regulated and trade is much more free. One problem is that not everyone accepts Cryptocurrency like they would accept dollars. You can only trade with people who also trade Cryptocurrency.

Since Cryptocurrency enables quite a few micro-financing options, it can also help start-ups raise capital by leveraging micro-financing. Just to make sure that there is no confusion, your company does not have to be a Cryptocurrency company. This option is simply to raise money by having the option to either take payment or donations in Cryptocurrency.

There are fundraising options available with Cryptocurrency that are not available if you want to raise dollars or deal with banks. When you raise money with dollars, you typically have to go through institutions like banks or investors, which require traction and a viable product. That makes traditional fundraising options very exclusive.

The same is true if you would like to become an early stage investor. It is a very difficult to do because it is difficult to get access to the best start-up companies in which you can invest. Again, there are many gatekeepers and lots of friction if you are a small player trying to get into that industry. Plus, there are many laws (if you are based in the United States) that prevent you from doing this.

With Cryptocurrency, this changes. You can sell stock of your company for Cryptocurrency. In the past, I've recommended specific websites for this, but since Cryptocurrency is very new, sites where you can buy and sell Cryptocurrency shares often become defunct and new ones pop up. So I suggest that you search Google for "Cryptocurrency stock exchange companies" and similar online searches, and see if it might be right for you.

Some Cryptocurrency stock exchange companies enable you to list your company on their site and sell shares of your company to real people for Cryptocurrency instead of dollars or any other government issued currency. You can then exchange that Cryptocurrency for dollars elsewhere. You can also use your Cryptocurrency to invest in other companies listed on those Cryptocurrency exchange websites.

Such Cryptocurrency exchange companies act as a public market such as the Nasdaq or the Dow Jones. But the companies that trade on these Cryptocurrency stock exchanges are typically small start-ups that need extra funding.

Average people browse listings on Cryptocurrency exchange companies to buy and sell their shares. If you are able to list your business on such exchanges, regular people can invest in your company using the Cryptocurrency.

If you are based in the United States, you have to be aware of the SEC rules and regulations to use sites like this. Make sure you research the rules for your particular business before you post your business on such websites. This is a new industry and the laws change very rapidly.

12. Bonus Two: Patreon

If you are already active in your business niche in any shape or form, you might have a group of people who already know about you and appreciate your work.

Patreon.com is a website where people can donate to others for their creative work. For example, if you already do blogging, create YouTube videos, run a podcast, or put out other types of content, your fans might give you donations to keep going.

Doing things like blogging, YouTubing, or podcasting will not only get you leads and customers, but with Patreon, it can also help you fundraise.

13. BONUS THREE: I can help you

You are welcome to email me with questions. Now that you have a sense of your options for raising money, email me at alex.genadinik@gmail.com with your initial fundraising strategy and I'll happily give you feedback.

In one or two sentences, tell me about your project, list the ways you are thinking to raise money. That way your email won't become too long, and I'll be able to reply. I'll try to steer you in the right direction and evaluate your overall business and your fundraising strategy. I look forward to helping you!

When you email me, please explain that you are reading this book. That will help me gain context and I'll do my best to prioritize your email as a reader of this book.

CHAPTER 3: CRAZY AND WEIRD WAYS TO RAISE MONEY

This chapter contains a few weird fundraising strategies. If you need a million dollars, these strategies won't help you. But if you need only a few thousand dollars for initial equipment, website development, marketing, or business registration costs, these strategies can be ideal for cobbling together cash from different sources to help you raise the amount needed to carry your business to a desired milestone.

1. Sell body parts (Not as crazy as it sounds!)

Selling body parts may sound scary, but many body parts like hair or sperm grow back in endless amounts and are painless for you to give.

Simply search Google for places near you where you can sell that in your local area, and you can begin raising extra cash. If you are not embarrassed to raise money this way, doing this will generate some quick cash.

Depending on how far you are willing to take this, it can be very profitable. One past client signed up to be a surrogate mother and carried a baby for nine months. It wasn't based on my advice; I would not advise going that far just to fund a business. It was a story she shared with me. She got paid tens of thousands of dollars for doing this, which was equivalent to her annual salary, and she was able to put that money into a business.

2. Medical and research study participation

You don't have to take weird new drugs that will make you grow a tale or an eleventh toe. Many universities have non-medical tests or experiments where they need people for study participation. Inquire in various university or hospital research labs near you, and get on lists for experiments. There may be easy cash in it for you. If you do experiment in studies of new medical drugs and do grow an eleventh toe, be sure to send a picture. You'll get the hustle prize.

3. Sell your junk and garage sale arbitrage

If you don't want to sell parts of your body, how about some items you have around your home? Consider selling items you no longer use from your home on sites like eBay and Craigslist. If you become good at selling things on these websites, you can even turn this into a mini side business by scouring local garage and estate sales for things you can resell and have that be a consistent source of revenue for you to boost your business until you get to ramen profitability or can raise a substantial amount.

If you become extremely good at re-selling things online, you can source products from a site like AliExpress that has thousands of products to choose from.

CHAPTER 4: BUSINESS FUNDAMENTALS AND COMMENTARY

1. Why it's not as easy as it seems to raise money from investors

Many entrepreneurs hope to get an investment from investors. When entrepreneurs see investor interviews on TV, YouTube, or social media, those investors often seem very friendly, open, warm, and approachable. It is a part of every investor's job to build a very positive public persona so they attract and a large flow of entrepreneurs hoping to receive money from them. That way they can have their choice of companies to choose from for their few investments.

Unfortunately, real one-on-one interactions with many of those same investors don't go as planned. From my own experience and from talking to many entrepreneurs, I have found this to be a common phenomenon.

To be clear, once an investor invests in your company, chances are that they will always be nice and professional. After all, that investor will be vested in your success and will/should do whatever is in their power to help you. The caveat, of course, if you do a bad job growing your company. In that case, your investors may not be too fond of you. But for now, let's focus on approaching investors who have not yet invested in your business, or have not even talked to you before.

The first meeting between an entrepreneur and an investor often happens when the entrepreneur simply approaches the investor for a conversation. Good investors get pitched by over a thousand entrepreneurs each year. They can tell rather quickly if they are interested or not. If the investor is not too interested, they usually try to wrap up the conversation swiftly to help everyone not waste their time. For the entrepreneur, on the other hand, this first meeting is a special opportunity since they don't get to talk to investors too often. When entrepreneurs try to unnaturally extend the duration of the meeting, the investor may get irritated.

Even though most investors only make a few investments per year, they have to see hundreds or thousands of entrepreneurs in a year. From those hundreds of entrepreneurs, the investors must choose only a handful of the very best companies. Meeting a few entrepreneurs is fun, but seeing so many companies can be very overwhelming. Those investors were once entrepreneurs themselves. It is enjoyable for experienced business people to help younger entrepreneurs. But if you are busy, and are seeing so many young entrepreneurs, the enjoyment quickly dissipates and seeing more entrepreneurs becomes slightly annoying. This is why investors often appear jaded and answer email messages with one-line replies if they reply at all.

As an entrepreneur, you must differentiate yourself from the hoards of others meeting with the same investor. There are a couple of common ways to make yourself stand out.

First, try not to ask for money or advice after just a few minutes of conversation. Investors know what you're after; hey know you are hungry for cash. You must try to remain authentic and engage with them in a stimulating way. They want to be intellectually stimulated instead of having to rehash conversations they've already had with hundreds of people before.

Being interesting or intelligent and not babbling or going on and on about your business is the simplest way to offer them value. There's also a fine line between confidence and ego, so my advice is to try to avoid coming off as a sycophant.

Second, be brief and on point. That comes from being prepared. Don't approach investors before your idea is fully flushed out, your pitch is succinct, and you have a specific ask. The ask can range from a simple question to an eventual investment. Just make sure not to just babble on and on. The investor's interest will correlate with the merit of your business. If you present something compelling, they may take interest. If your idea doesn't impress them, they might quickly lose interest because they've likely heard many similar ideas before.

One good practice is to find investors who invest in the kind of company that you are trying to grow or the industry in which your business is in. When you can, try to get introductions to those investors through your contacts in that industry. One of the best ways to get their attention is through introductions by people the investors already work with. You can get such introductions from other entrepreneurs who already work at companies that those investors have invested in. Introductions are much more effective ways of getting an investor's attention that sending them cold emails or randomly approaching them on social media.

Getting introductions isn't an easy strategy because the

entrepreneurs who work with them may not immediately want to recommend someone they just met to an investor whose respect they want to keep, but this is precisely why investors want recommendations. Investors must create a barrier to access to them because they need to make sure that their time is spent talking only to entrepreneurs who are growing great companies and can be trusted.

2. Examples of starting different types of businesses with less money

When entrepreneurs start their businesses, they often have grand plans, which can require substantial amounts of money. Since it is difficult to raise money, you must consider keeping the grand, long-term vision but temporarily scaling down the grand plans for the business so that it can get started within a reasonable budget that is easier to raise. Once you get started, if you are successful, you will eventually grow into all your grand plans. But first thing is first. You must actually get started. It is often possible to greatly reduce start up costs. Let's examine a few different types of businesses and explore some strategies for reducing their funding needs.

ONLINE BUSINESSES

Many people grossly overestimate how much money

they need when they want to start an online business. People often think that they either have to spend a lot of money building a website, or if they plan to sell something, they think that they need to buy/create large quantities of inventory up-front. Luckily, there are practical approaches to both of these challenges. You can create your own website by yourself in just a few days, for nearly free using WordPress. I have a specific tutorial for this, which shows you how to set up your website quickly and even get a free domain name. You can see the tutorial on my website by visiting this URL:

http://www.problemio.com/website.html

If you don't want to bother working on your website or feel intimidated by it, you can have a professional website created for you by a great freelancer. Use the website UpWork.com to find freelancers who can set up a WordPress website for you in a day or two, for $100-200 max. If you don't have a good domain name in mind or still feel lost, you can email me with specific questions at:

alex.genadinik@gmail.com

I'll do my best to advise the best approach for you after I understand what you are hoping to accomplish. In some cases, I work with clients on helping them find a great domain name, set up their website, and get it ready for promotion.

If you plan to sell products on your site, you often do not

need to make an up-front purchase of the inventory you plan to sell. You can simply sign up to be an affiliate of Amazon or affiliate reseller on sites like cj.com (formerly CommissionJunction), and resell products made by other companies. If you get credited for a sale as an affiliate reseller, you will be paid a commission. This is a great way to start such a business because you do not need to risk money by buying inventory, shipping items, handling logistics, or anything else. All you need to do is sell. Once you are able to sell a significant volume of products, it is less risky to consider owning some of the inventory to be able to collect a larger portion of the sales.

Another way to avoid having to buy a significant amount of inventory up-front is to use a site like AliExpress.com which is owned by the same company as Alibaba.com. Most people are familiar with Alibaba. It is a site where you can buy a significant amount of inventory up-front in order to get a cheaper price per unit. That is risky because it requires a significant financial investment. AliExpress solves this problem by allowing you to buy the inventory one product at a time.

FASHION DESIGN AND CLOTHING (OR OTHER PRODUCT) MANUFACTURING

Another kind of business where people make the mistake of overestimating the amount of money they need to get started are fashion related businesses. Many entrepreneurs immediately want to produce a large batch of the clothing they design. They typically skip a number of steps in the overall business process. For example, before a piece of clothing should be manufactured in mass, there should be testing of how well that piece of clothing sells. You can do sales on a small scale online or simply by setting up a cart or a stand or selling at flea markets or other relevant events in your local city. This will give you an initial test to see which of the items you designed and created sell best. If one of your designs sells extremely well, it justifies bigger tests. If you don't see positive signs from your initial tests, it is likely a sign that you need to go back to the drawing board and improve the product before it is ready for mass production. After you improve the product, you must run the same tests on a small scale to see whether you get more positive results. The problem with producing a large batch of clothing is that if it doesn't sell well, you will be stuck with all that inventory you can't sell and you're out all that money. A similar scenario is true with other kinds of products that you must manufacture. You should test your sales channels before you take the risk of manufacturing a large batch of products if there is no certainty that the products will sell.

As you test sales channels and find designs that sell well, the next step is to establish predictable and consistent marketing channels for them. This can generate enough revenue to fund bigger and bigger batches of clothing that you can produce.

I want to share an additional case study. One aspiring entrepreneur I know who wanted to create his own

T-shirt design company started out by getting a job at a T-shirt print shop. That gave him a salary and the ability to print his own T-shirts after the print shop's closing hours (with the consent of the owner). This way he was able to get the clothing made cheaply while maintaining two sources of income: his job and sales of his T-shirts. He had less stress, unlimited financial runway during which to make his business succeed, some mentorship from current shop owners, and he was able to run more experiments to find designs that sell well. He didn't wait around for money to fall into his lap. He was resourceful, worked hard, got a strategic job that was in essence his funder and mentor, and eventually succeeded. If he waited for money to come from other sources, he might still be waiting to start his business. Instead, he proactively went after his dream. Over time, he perfected his T-shirt designs and was able to save enough money to open his own print shop that he now successfully runs.

RESTAURANT

It is extremely difficult to start a restaurant and turn it into a success. While there are ways to decrease costs, it is almost never cheap. It is important to understand that there is an extremely high failure rate for such a business. You must surround yourself with very good advisors who have started restaurants in the past. Prior to opening your restaurant, you must understand the most common causes of failure for restaurants and have a solid plan to overcome those challenges. Don't rush into starting this kind of a business. Instead, learn as much as possible about owning and running a restaurant before you open one. This is one of the most difficult businesses there is. Make sure you know what you are getting into before you do.

If you do open a restaurant, you can save money by buying an existing space where there was a restaurant before. It will save money on renovations to create the kitchen and much of the remodeling. The challenge is that this kind of a business has many different costs and you must be savvy about cutting most of them without cutting the quality of the restaurant.

One way to get into the food business in a more reasonable way is to start a food truck or a food cart. They require much less money, and you can see if it's even something you want to do long-term. These are not ideal options for someone who wants to open a restaurant, but for this business, it is hard to start small.

SERVICE-BASED LOCAL BUSINESSES

Many kinds of businesses fall into the category of local services. These can be chiropractors, doctors, roofers, painters, cleaners, mechanics, mobile services that come to your home to perform some service, and many other kinds of businesses that serve clients within a local geographic area. These businesses have a few things in common. Before starting them, many entrepreneurs get caught up in the costs of opening an office, buying equipment, remodeling, hiring staff, and registering the business with the state.

While it is nearly impossible to get around large start-up costs with some types of local businesses like restaurants, many local service businesses do not have to have significant costs to get started.

All local business entrepreneurs face a similar dilemma. They must invest quite a bit of money into their business before even being in a position to launch and get their first clients. I am not a fan of taking that much risk! Plus, getting the money to start the business can take months or even years if the entrepreneur doesn't already have that money.

To solve that challenge, there is one controversial strategy that might work for many types of local businesses. What some entrepreneurs do is start promoting their business before the business is operational. The purpose of this is to see if the business can get clients or inbound phone calls before risking money and time investing in the business. If people do start calling to make an appointment, you can simply tell them that the business is not taking new clients at the moment, and that you would be happy to put that potential customer on the waiting list and call them when the business is ready to take on new customers. This somewhat controversial strategy helps to take the risk out of starting the business because it lets you explore and build marketing channels. Once you find marketing channels that consistently bring you potential clients, you can at least be assured that you will have some client base to begin with. Plus, this gives you something to do for your business while you are waiting for either funds or business licenses.

This strategy is not for the faint of heart and for a variety of reasons, most people tend to be worried about pursuing it. I wouldn't recommend you pursue this strategy. I simply leave it up to you to decide whether it is something that makes sense for you to decrease your risk and costs to start your business.

TECHNOLOGY COMPANIES

If you want to start a technology business or a software start-up, you must follow the Lean Startup methodology by Eric Ries. This is an industry standard, and a way for you to spend minimal company resources while creating the best product possible.

The mistake many first-time tech entrepreneurs make is starting with a big vision and trying to launch with that big vision. As you can imagine, it is expensive and time consuming to pursue from the beginning. The projects become bulky with requirements, get bogged down somewhere in the process, and often never even get launched.

The Lean Startup methodology is a very different approach. It suggests that you identify something called a minimum viable product (MVP), and launch with that. Once you launch your MVP, you will be able to put that product in the hands of potential customers and get their feedback. You can talk to them about whether they would buy it, and ask why not if they say they wouldn't. Once you talk to a number of people and gather feedback, the Lean Startup methodology dictates that you improve your product based on the feedback you got. Once you make those suggested improvements, show people the new and improved version of your product, and again, ask potential customers what they like and don't like about the product.

You should have many such rapid cycles of improving your product and gathering feedback. Each cycle will boost your product quality. This process helps you quickly evolve and improve your product with minimal wasted effort and minimal guessing of what your customers will want. Doing this will save you money and time.

FOOD PRODUCTS

Many people love to cook and experiment with food. There are many aspiring food entrepreneurs who think their latest concoction can be the next big popular food product. Unfortunately, creating a new food item is an extremely difficult business. Big grocery stores make new food companies jump through large hurdles to get placed on their shelves. Even when they do, the store buys items at very low prices while adding many requirements like fancy and expensive packaging and for you to allocate some of your own money for marketing. Small stores have different challenges than bigger grocery stores do. Small grocery stores simply don't sell enough products to make a big financial impact for you. Plus, they don't have much shelf space for your new products. Selling new foods wholesale to restaurants and other companies is another difficult option as you have to start contacting different small businesses and engage in a very serious outreach and sales process.

If you feel that you have a winning new food item, in order to build your business sustainably and cheaply, consider selling it on your own either online if possible, or by building a small local following and establishing your own sales/marketing channels. It will take you a while, but you can do this with organic growth, which won't require you to raise any money. Keep gaining local recognition. Depending on what your food item is, that might even evolve into a successful catering or a food truck business. As you gain momentum and revenue, it will be easier to raise money to expand your business.

If your food product is something that can be shipped, you can sell your food product online through sites that allow food sales like Amazon or through your own website. Recall that you can create your own simple but professional website using WordPress and get up and running quickly.

Here's a checklist to reduce costs for your business:

1) See how you can get up and running quickly
2) Launch fast
3) Establish sales/marketing channels

4) Improve product over time

5) Grow into your bigger vision rather than launching with it

3. Raising money accomplishes far less than entrepreneurs think

Many entrepreneurs think that if they were just able to raise money, that would be enough to help them turn their business into a success. Money helps, but money alone is not nearly as useful as people imagine it to be. Money has a way of running out quickly and being spent in suboptimal ways. I want to share my own experience of raising money to illustrate why money isn't as helpful as it seems.

Many years ago I was working on my first real start-up. That company eventually failed mostly due to my inexperience, but regardless it taught me lessons about raising money. During the very early stages of building that business, I was trying to raise from $25,000 to $50,000, which is a reasonable amount for a seed round investment. I had met an investor and pitched him my business. He didn't invest because he saw that I was too much of a beginner, and my business idea didn't appeal to him either. I was very disappointed. I felt that if only I had gotten the money I needed, that money could have funded the company for a few months by helping me and my co-founders pay rent and cover business expenses. To me, that would have been enough to make that business a success.

Since I didn't get that money from an investor, I went ahead with the business anyway. I dipped into my savings to help the company move forward and all of us worked for free instead of having a small salary from the potential seed investment. It was very stressful to work without income. Ultimately, the amount of work we put into the business was orders of magnitude more than the initial investment would have been. And what do you think happened? First of all, the amount of time we needed to create a serious company was much more than the money I was seeking would have provided. I grossly underestimated the needs of the business. Second, even after double or triple the time and effort I thought the company needed, the company was still in nascent stages due partially to my poor management and partly to me not understanding the business landscape. Looking back, I realize that the money I thought would have been so helpful would have simply been wasted and I would have been in the same situation as I was without getting the investment. That money would not have made any difference in the business. It would have alleviated much of my stress, but an investor isn't paying to relieve my stress.

This story has two takeaways. The first is that getting an investment is not nearly as helpful as entrepreneurs think it will be. Without a great business strategy and direction, the money runs out pretty quickly and fruitlessly. The second lesson is that if someone on my team had significant business experience and steered me and the company in the right direction, that would have helped the company survive much more than cash ever would have. One big mistake can take months to recover from. A good advisor can help you avoid many such mistakes, and is arguably more valuable than money during the initial stages of the business. It might be better to spend your efforts looking for a good mentor or an advisor rather than raising money.

It will be more difficult in the short-term without the cash, but your business will have a far greater chance of success if you get a great mentor or an advisor.

4. Drawbacks of raising money

Many entrepreneurs raising money tend to focus mostly on the benefits of raising money rather than the drawbacks. There are many potential disadvantages that come with the fundraising process. Let's take a few moments to explore some.

LOANS: THEY MUST BE PAID BACK

If you are considering funding your business by taking out a personal or business loan, keep in mind that when you take a loan, that money isn't yours. You must pay that money back. If your business doesn't succeed, not only will you have a failed business, but you will also be stuck paying off the loan. That's almost like losing that money twice.

Entrepreneurs tend to be optimistic and think that failure isn't something that will happen to them, but statistically, most businesses fail. You must evaluate scenarios where your business does not succeed. Doing this will help you understand the amount of risk you add when you take out a loan to fund your business.

SIMPLY TAKING CASH WON'T HELP YOU NEARLY AS MUCH AS YOU THINK

Cash has a way of getting spent quickly and running out. If your business direction and strategy are not optimal, you may end up spending the money pursuing bad business strategies, which will ultimately drive your business into a dead end. It's an awful feeling to realize that the business strategies you were executing for all those months were faulty, and you've spend most of your cash pursuing them, and ultimately didn't end up growing your business nearly as much as you had hoped.

Prioritize finding great mentors, advisers, and experienced co-founders rather than simply getting cash.

MEDDLING INVESTORS

If you are lucky enough to get an investment, that may seem like a huge boost for your business. But there are some investors who add a negative presence to the business and want to influence direction more than they should. Some investors are also too concerned about their money in the short term, and don't understand that they made a long-term investment. Those investors can annoy you and waste your time by calling you daily or weekly to check on the progress of your company. That may seem okay in exchange for taking their money, but if their meddling presence begins to have a negative impact on various parts of the business, how much does their money really help?

INVESTORS WHO WON'T LET YOU RUN YOUR COMPANY

Some investors (especially non-professional ones) think that since they gave you money, they have a strong say in business direction, and exert pressure on you to do what they say. Don't forget that this is ultimately your business. It is great to take advice, but you must make the final decisions. Before accepting investment from anyone, make sure you set their expectations on how much you expect them to contribute and in what facets of the business.

WASTING TIME FUNDRAISING

One of the worst things about raising money is spending a lot of your resources (time, money, and emotional energy) and not ultimately raising any money. That represents a complete waste of your time, which you could have put into the growth of your business or improving your product.

Think twice before you begin your fundraising efforts. Consider how likely you are to succeed pursuing the fundraising strategies you are about to explore. Think about whether these efforts will be worth the risk, and whether it might be better to put those efforts into your actual business.

PITFALLS OF TAKING MONEY FROM FAMILY

Taking money from loving family or friends might sometimes be a simple and available option, but getting into business partnerships and financial dealings with family has a way of adding a potentially negative new dimension to your personal relationships. Be very careful, as you might not want to jeopardize those relationships. Family and friends are more important than business. Plus, think about how hard your family and friends worked to earn the money they might give you. Taking money from friends and family has ethical and moral implications.

CHAPTER 5: MAKING MONEY ONLINE TO PUT TOWARD YOUR BUSINESS AS A FUNDRAISING SOURCE

1. Thought leadership and immediate early revenue

Whatever your business is, it would behoove you to position yourself and your business as authoritative as possible within your industry. You can accomplish that by hosting a podcast, a YouTube show, writing a book, maintaining a popular blog, or by creating a course teaching something within your industry that your potential clients might want to learn.

Doing these things can help you generate early revenue that you can put toward your business in addition to giving you industry authority. In fact, if you are considering getting into an industry you are not 100% sure about, the options I just mentioned can be easy ways to enter an industry. These platforms don't require a lot of time or money to launch (except a book, if you overthink it and approach it as a perfectionist). You can also use all of them as marketing to funnel leads toward your business.

Just keep in mind that none of these usually succeed at first. It almost always takes persistence and long-term consistent effort to improve your craft at whatever you choose to pursue to make money. Be patient with these strategies if at first they don't succeed.

2. Cheap consultations as lead generation

Another way to generate income for your business can be to do coaching or consulting in your industry. While it might be somewhat rare to get high-paying clients, a good solution might be to do discounted coaching. The discounts will get you early clients you might not otherwise have gotten, and that revenue can be put toward the money you need to launch or sustain your main business. Plus, this tactic will help you establish business relationships within your industry.

3. How to earn 1,000% more revenue per client

Keep the following strategies in mind for the main business you are planning, and for your hustle strategies to generate revenue toward your business from a blog, podcast, YouTube channel, book, course, coaching or consulting.

While making 1,000% more from clients might sound too good to be true, doing so is easier than you might think, and if you do it correctly, your clients will even appreciate it if you give them more than 1,000% the value for their money. There are common strategies to boost customer LTV (lifetime value). Most of these strategies focus on retaining your customers for longer periods of time by making them love your product or service by wowing them with quality. Here is a brief overview of ways you can generate hundreds, and in some cases thousands, of percent from the same clients:

i. Sell consumable products: Think of food, clothing, digital goods or content. Once people consume one, if they like it, they will be keen on getting another. That's an immediate 100% revenue boost. If they keep liking what you sell and buy another and another, that same client can soon spend 1,000% or more on your business.

Picture yourself shopping in a supermarket. Imagine buying a yogurt. If you don't like that yogurt, you won't buy it again. The company who made it, earned only a little bit of money from you. It is good for them. But imagine if you liked that yogurt and decided to have it for breakfast every day. That is 365 times that you could buy that yogurt this year. If you liked that yogurt enough to eat it as an afternoon snack and tried different flavors, you could buy over 500 packages of that same yogurt within a year. That is a tremendous difference, which would generate that yogurt company 500 times more money if their yogurt quality was amazing. That is a 500,000% difference in sales from one customer.

ii. Anything subscription-based: If people know that they like your products and want to get more of them, you can offer them at a discount if they subscribe to get whatever they are consuming regularly. Having people subscribed will decrease the chance of them getting distracted and forgetting to come back to your business. Even if they forget about your business, the subscription will still charge them on a regular basis.

If people buy a monthly subscription, they will buy 1,200% more of your products this year compared to if they just bought once and forgot about your business.

iii. Catalog model: If you sell one thing, why not sell many types or variations of the same thing? When you go to a store, you often see food you like in different flavors. You might want to try all the flavors, and you might often get one of each flavor, immediately spending hundreds of percent more.

If we consider the same yogurt example, we might want to try the cherry flavor, strawberry, blueberry, vanilla, and so on. But wait, the yogurts are in a catalog of all dairy products. Next to the yogurt is the milk, buttermilk, half and half, and so on. As we browse the dairy product section, we might also end up buying dairy products that aren't yogurt, and that's the real power of the catalog model.

iv. Quality: If people like your product, they will naturally come back for more.

v. Cultivate super customers: People who love you will recommend you to friends and come back for more of what you offer. This is done with great product quality and great customer care and support.

vi. Upsells: Have upsells in mind you know are natural for the client to need/want at some point after the initial service. When selling one service, have additional things to offer your clients. Even if you can't provide that up-sell yourself, you can recommend another company for a referral or a commission fee.

For example, if you are looking to raise money for your business, I can assume that you are starting a business. And if you are reading one book, I can assume that you may enjoy learning by reading. Very naturally, I can offer you additional business products or books that you may enjoy. An example of such a product is my very popular business plan book. I link to all my books and a number of free resources at the end of this book. Be careful to only do such things if it is a perfect fit for your client's needs. Otherwise, you will run the risk of irritating them and losing them as a long-term customer.

vii. Build sharing and recommendations into your product. Allow your product to be used with a friend, or leverage discounts and recommendation incentives to get people to recommend your product or service to people they know. These simple strategies will turn your customers into very willing marketers of your product or services. As long as there is benefit for your customers to share, they will. Your job is to create an incentive for them to share.

4. Freelancing online on UpWork and Fiverr

What are your thoughts on my earlier suggestion that you consider getting a part-time job to fund your business? This suggestion is back in this section, but in a different manifestation.

You can make extra money that can be put toward your business if you freelance online. Common online freelancing sites are Fiverr.com and UpWork.com. Most of the freelancing there is in tech/programming/marketing/design space, but even if you don't have those skills, you can do something simpler or less technical.

This isn't the easiest or most attractive way to get money, but sometimes getting cash for your business is all about hustling and not thinking that you are too good to get your hands dirty doing work that may be considered somewhat humbling.

5. Local service as a local concierge or assistant

While you can do freelancing online, you can also do freelance work in your local area as a local assistant, sometimes called a local concierge. If you live in the U.S. or Europe, you can command higher rates with local clients than clients online from freelancing sites. That's because online you might have to compete with people who live in countries where the cost of living is much lower, so they can charge much lower rates.

An example of a local concierge site is TaskRabbit.com or you can simply promote your services on general local services websites like CraigsList.com, Yelp.com or YellowPages.com.

THE END!

EPILOGUE

Getting money for your business is not easy. As you see, most of the strategies to raise money have little or no overlap with the highest priority tasks that need to be done to move your business forward. As much as you can, move your business forward despite having limited financial resources. Don't forget that most of the time, resourcefulness, hustle and creativity can get you further than money. And never allow not having money to become an excuse for not moving your business forward. When there is a will, there's a way. Make that your theme, and you will succeed.

FUN FUNDRAISING FACTS

1) Nearly all people who put their savings into their business quit spending their savings before the sum of money they allotted runs out. People see their savings whittling away, don't see enough progress in the business, and cut their losses.

2) There is a very small middle ground of people who spend the exact amount they allotted and stop. People who tend to continue tend to have elements of addiction, recklessness, embarrassment of failing, or another external pressure too great for the entrepreneur to quit. In such situations, many entrepreneurs have become obsessive and run through their entire savings.

3) When you are in a bad financial situation, it can cause consistent stress over a long period of time. Stress impacts the same part of the brain that deals with the fight or flight instinct. This part of the brain is called the Amygdala. When the Amygdala takes over, our brains focus on removing the immediate source of the stress. This translates to short-term thinking and decisions aimed at removing the source of the stress, and inhibits our ability for long-term thinking. Having an overwhelmingly short-term business focus can lead us to make many mistakes in what we focus on and how we choose to run our business.

Now that you know this, focus on decreasing your stress with exercise, proper diet, mindfulness of your thoughts and reactions, and by getting enough sleep. This will help you avoid short-term thinking which will work to get you out of your financial stress faster.

4) My estimate is that 99% of today's online businesses can be started without any investment for under $1,000 and in many cases much less if the founders are willing to learn new skills, and the founding team is properly chosen to include the core skills needed by the business.

FURTHER FREE RESOURCES

Gift 1: One free online business or marketing course of your choosing

I teach over 100 online courses on business and marketing. For being a reader of this book, you get access to one course absolutely free. You just have to choose which one. Browse my full list of courses, email me (alex.genadinik@gmail.com) which course you want, and I will send you a free coupon!

Here is my full list of courses:

https://www.udemy.com/user/alexgenadinik/

Gift: 2: Get my iPhone and Android business apps for free

My apps come as a 4-app series on iPhone and Android. I have free versions of each!

Here are shortened links for convenience:

Free Android business plan app:
https://goo.gl/GDl0TB

Free Android marketing app:
https://goo.gl/jhsWt6

Free Android app on fundraising and making money:
https://goo.gl/BcAX60

Free Android business idea app:
https://goo.gl/niEjaH

Free iPhone business plan app:
https://goo.gl/VBWtsC

Free iPhone marketing app:
https://goo.gl/8l112P

Free iPhone app for fundraising and making money:
https://goo.gl/WO1L53

Free iPhone business idea iPhone app:
https://goo.gl/eyKEzT

Gift 3: Free business advice

If you have questions about your business or anything mentioned in this book, email me and I will be happy to advise you over email. Just please keep two things in mind:

1) Remind me that you purchased this book.
2) Please make your questions clear and concise. I love to help, but I am often overwhelmed with work unfortunately have limited time.

Gift 4: **More free products**

When I have free promotions for my products, the four places I post them are my YouTube channel, email list, Twitter, and Facebook group. If you subscribe, you will get future updates about free products. Just keep in mind that I promote everything and anything business related on my social media accounts so it won't just be the freebies.

Sign up for my email list:

http://glowingstart.com/email-subscribe/

My YouTube channel:

http://www.youtube.com/user/Okudjavavich

My Facebook group:

https://www.facebook.com/groups/problemio/

You can also follow me on Twitter @genadinik

COMPLETE LIST OF MY BOOKS

If you enjoyed this book, check out my Amazon author page to see the full list of my books:

https://goo.gl/CA5Tzn

All my books can also be found on my website:

http://www.problemio.com

ABOUT THE AUTHOR

Alex Genadinik is a successful serial entrepreneur, software engineer, and a marketer. Alex is the creator of the Problemio.com business apps, which are some of the top mobile apps for planning and starting a business with 2,000,000+ downloads across iOS, Android, and Kindle. In addition to the mobile apps, Alex is the author of many popular books and online courses on how to start and grow a business. Alex has a B.S in Computer Science from San Jose State University.

Made in the USA
San Bernardino, CA
23 December 2018